Collins

easy learning

English

Ages 7–9

quick quizzes

Comprehension: fiction

Read the text to find an answer to each question.

There were six young colts in the meadow besides me; they were older than I was; some were nearly as large as grown-up horses. I used to run with them, and had great fun; we used to gallop all together round and round the field, as hard as we could go. Sometimes we had rather rough play, for they would frequently bite and kick as well as gallop.

One day, when there was a good deal of kicking, my mother whinnied to me to come to her, and then she said:

'I wish you to pay attention to what I am going to say to you. The colts who live here are very good colts, but they are cart-horse colts, and, of course, they have not learned manners. You have been well bred and well born; your father has a great name in these parts, and your grandfather won the cup two years at the Newmarket races; your grandmother had the sweetest temper of any horse I ever knew, and I think you have never seen me kick or bite. I hope you will grow up gentle and good, and never learn bad ways; do your work with a good will, lift your feet up well when you trot, and never bite or kick even in play.'

From *Black Beauty* by Anna Sewell

1 This story is written in the first person. Who or what is telling the story? _____

2 How many young colts (male horses) were there in the meadow altogether?

_____

3 In line 3, what does "gallop" mean?

_____

4 What "bad ways" was Black Beauty's mother worried he would learn from the cart-horse colts?

_____

5 What sort of horse was Black Beauty's grandfather?

_____

6 Black Beauty's grandmother had "the sweetest temper". What does 'sweet' mean here?

_____

Colour your score

2

Common exception words

Circle the correctly spelt word.

Exception words don't follow the usual spelling rules and patterns.

1 I ride my **bicycle / bycicle** to the park after school.

2 There are a hundred years in a **sentury / century**.

3 I **believe / beleve** in fairies.

4 I took a deep **breathe / breath** before diving into the pool.

5 I had a **strange / straynge** dream last night.

6 I need to return my book to the **library / libary**.

7 We have a **separate / seperate** bin for our recycling.

8 My birthday is in **Febuary / February**.

9 There were two **woman / women** standing at the bus stop.

10 David Walliams is my **favourite / faverite** author.

11 We listened carefully for the correct **anser / answer**.

12 There are 60 seconds in a **minute / minite**.

13 A fierce dog stood on **gard / guard** at the front gate.

14 The **notise / notice** said "No ball games".

15 Crete is a Greek **island / ireland**.

Colour your score

3

Consonants and vowels

Circle the consonant letters.

1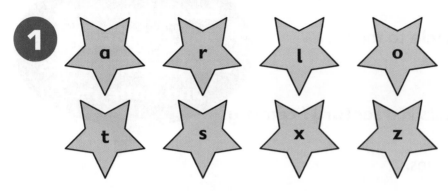

a r l o

t s x z

Vowel sounds can be represented by vowels, y or groups of letters.

Circle the vowel letters.

2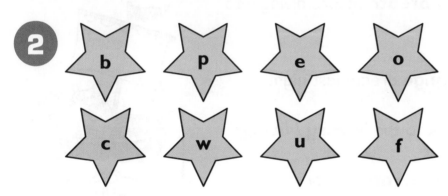

b p e o

c w u f

Underline the letter(s) that stand for the vowel sound in each word.

3 play

4 grey

5 fly

6 brain

7 bright

8 snow

9 stretch

10 through

11 tweet

12 bread

13 mouth

14 myth

15 vein

Colour your score

A or an?

Write **a** or **an** before each animal.

1 ____ meerkat

2 ____ tortoise

3 ____ orangutan

4 ____ squirrel

5 ____ gorilla

6 ____ anteater

7 ____ elephant

8 ____ yak

9 ____ hippopotamus

10 ____ iguana

Write **a** or **an** in each space.

11 My uncle is ____ heavyweight boxer.

12 My aunt is ____ estate agent.

13 My dad is ____ librarian.

14 My sister works in ____ animal rescue centre.

15 My grandpa used to be ____ pilot.

Use **an** before words that start with a vowel sound.

Colour your score

15
14
13
12
11
10
9
8
7
6
5
4
3
2
1

Direct speech

Copy each sentence and add speech punctuation.

1 Abracadabra shouted the magician.

_____

_____

2 May I take your order asked the waiter.

_____

_____

3 The runner said I've got a blister.

_____

4 There's no place like home said Dorothy.

_____

_____

5 Her brother yelled Go away!

_____

6 Tom asked Have you seen my car keys?

_____

_____

7 I'd like to go home said the little boy.

_____

_____

8 Bonjour said Martine.

_____

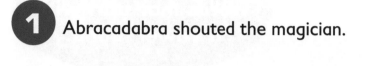

Remember to use a punctuation mark before the closing speech marks.

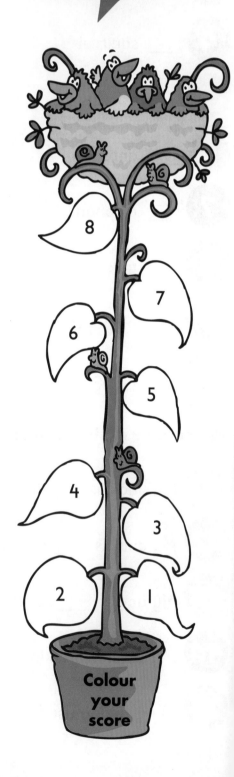

8
7
6
5
4
3
2
1

Colour your score

Choosing the best word

Circle the best word in bold to complete each sentence.

Choose the words that are most precise in meaning.

1 Your dad is very **long / towering / tall**.

2 Cars must **end / stop / cease** at a red light.

3 The princess **lifted / elevated / raised** the crown carefully onto her head.

4 I chose the dog that was wagging its tail because he seemed very **kind / friendly / helpful**.

5 "We've won!" Mum **shouted / whispered / muttered**.

6 I love **cooking / frying / baking** cakes.

7 My dog has a **brief / short / concise** tail.

8 Please would you **increase / elevate / expand** my pocket money?

9 My French teacher helped me **convert / transfer / translate** the poem into English.

10 Please would you **borrow / lend / share** me some money to buy a drink?

11 Our clothes were **stained / demolished / sprinkled** with mud.

12 The lorry was too wide for the **narrow / slim / skinny** alley.

Colour your score

7

Pronouns

Write a suitable pronoun in each space.

1 Our car has broken down so _____ have postponed our outing.

2 I thought I had lost my calculator but I found _____ under my bed.

3 James was late for school because _____ didn't hear the alarm clock.

4 Mum had the fright of her life when _____ went on the ghost train.

5 Penguins can't fly but _____ are very good swimmers.

6 Dad won't let me have any pudding until _____ have eaten my dinner.

7 My brother and I were so helpful that Mum decided to take _____ to the cinema.

8 Although mosquitoes are tiny, _____ can do a lot of harm.

9 The shoes had holes in the soles so Mum threw _____ away.

10 There was a mouse in our kitchen until our cat chased _____ away.

Pronouns can be used in place of nouns to avoid repetition.

Colour your score

10 9 8 7 6 5 4 3 2 1

First or third person?

Read each sentence and write whether it is written using the **first** or the **third** person.

1 I am looking forward to lunchtime.

_____

2 Sam is cleaning out the guinea pigs' hutch.

_____

3 We are hoping to go for a swim later. _____

4 The school is celebrating its centenary.

_____

5 Our house is the oldest in the village. _____

6 Koalas are native to Australia. _____

7 The girls are playing hockey. _____

8 It is up to us to prove we can win! _____

9 I came third in the sack race. _____

10 They both enjoy karate. _____

11 My cat's name is Florrie. _____

12 Four children in my class have food allergies.

_____

Use **I**, **we**, **me** and **us** when writing in the first person.

Colour your score

Biography

Read Albert's account of his early life.
Circle the words in bold that tell his story in the third person.

He, she and they are used for writing in the third person.

I / Albert was born in 1911, in Dorset. **His / My** father, Jack, was a farm labourer. **His / My** mother died when **he / I** was just twelve years old. A few years later, **Albert / I** joined the army and met a young lady called Rose at the picture house. **We / They** married at the age of eighteen and moved into a farm cottage. **They / We** had six children although **their / our** second son died tragically from measles.

Times were hard for **us / Albert and his family**; there was no running water, no electricity and no gas. All **their / our** water had to be carried from a well in the back yard. One of the worst jobs was emptying the bucket from the outdoor lavatory, which was down a long path with spiders all round it. When the bucket was full, **we / they** had to dig a hole and bury the contents.

When war broke out, **Albert / I** had to leave immediately to join the army. **I remember / He remembers** walking up the hill, turning and waving. Rose and the little ones were crying. She wrote often with news of the children during **my / Albert's** four years in France. "My Albie" she called **him / me**.

Colour your score

Alphabetical order

Put these words in **alphabetical order.**

1 puzzle   ostrich   quarter

_____   _____   _____

2 octopus   otter   newt

_____   _____   _____

3 yawn   yolk   yogurt

_____   _____   _____

4 whistle   weather   whale

_____   _____   _____

5 bonfire   bottom   borrow

_____   _____   _____

6 suitcase   supper   sunflower

_____   _____   _____

7 motorbike   mirror   money

_____   _____   _____

8 insect   ingredient   iceberg

_____   _____   _____

9 Australia   America   Algeria

_____   _____   _____

10 kettle   kennel   kitten

_____   _____   _____

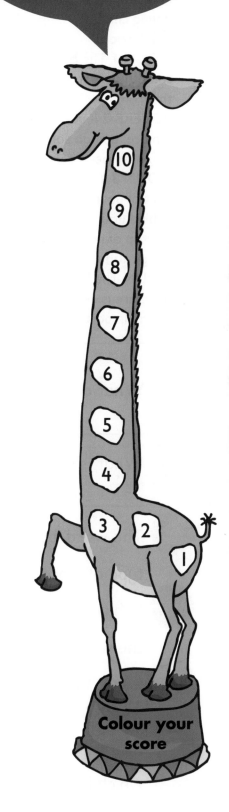

When words begin with the same letter(s), look at the next letter.

10
9
8
7
6
5
4
3   2
1

Colour your score

Using a dictionary

Use the dictionary page to find an answer to each question.

Bb

baby babies
NOUN A baby is a very young child.

back backs
NOUN 1 The **back** of something is the part opposite the front.
ADVERB 2 If you go **back** to a place, you go somewhere you have been before.
NOUN 3 Your **back** is the part of your body which is behind you, from your neck to the top of your legs.

background backgrounds
NOUN The **background** of a picture is everything behind the main part.

backwards
ADVERB 1 If you move **backwards**, you move with your back facing in the direction you are going.
ADVERB 2 If you do something **backwards**, you do it in the opposite of the usual way. *Let's try counting* **backwards** *from one hundred.*

bacon
NOUN **bacon** is salted meat from a pig.

bacteria
PLURAL NOUN **bacteria** are very tiny living things which break down waste. They can cause diseases.

bad worse, worst
ADJECTIVE 1 You say somebody is **bad** if they are naughty or wicked.
ADJECTIVE 2 If something is **bad**, it can hurt or upset you in some way.

badge badges
NOUN A badge is a sign people wear to show they belong to a school or club.

badger badgers
NOUN A **badger** is a strongly built animal with short legs and neck. It has long grey fur with a striped head.

---

1 What does a badger look like?

_____

2 What is a badge?

_____

3 The word 'back' can be used as a noun. What other type of word can it be used as? _____

4 Which headword (word in green) appears before the word 'bacon'? _____

5 Circle the word that is most likely to come after 'badger': **barbecue, cabbage, badminton, bicycle.**

6 If the word 'backgammon' is added to the dictionary, which headword will it come after? _____

Colour your score

Comprehension: non-fiction

Read the text to find an answer to each question.

Snake Bite!

Snakes have no ears, but they have an excellent sense of smell which makes them expert hunters. They use their forked tongues to pick up the scent of other animals.

All snakes are carnivores but the way in which they kill their prey differs depending on the type of snake. Some snakes are constrictors; they coil their long bodies around their victims and squeeze so tightly that the animal cannot breathe. Other snakes kill their prey with venom. Some snakes' venom is strong enough to kill a human. It takes effect very quickly so that the animal can't escape. The venom is stored in sacs close to the snake's long, sharp fangs. When the snake strikes, it sticks its deadly fangs into its prey, injecting venom into the animal and killing it quickly.

1 Which body part do snakes not have? _____

2 How do snakes find their prey?

_____

3 What is a carnivore?

_____

4 How does a constrictor kill its prey?

_____

5 What is venom?

_____

6 Where is a snake's venom stored?

_____

7 How do snakes inject their venom?

_____

8 Which adjective is used to show how dangerous a

snake bite can be? _____

Colour your score

Locating information

Use the index to find answers to the questions.

A
Aldrin, Edwin 10–11, 12
Apollo spacecraft 10–11, 12
Armstrong, Neil 10–11, 12
asteroid 4
astronaut 10–11, 12, 12, 18, 22–23
B
Big Bang 3
black hole 4
C
comet 9, 15
constellation 15, 16–17
D
diet (of astronauts) 12, 13
E
Earth 8–9
eclipse 10
G
galaxy 14–15
gravity 8, 12, 18, 22–23

J
Jupiter 8–9
M
Mars 8–9
Mercury 8–9
Meteor 15
Milky Way 14–15
Moon 8–9, 10
N
Neptune 8–9
O
orbit 2, 17
P
Peake, Tim 22–23
phases of Moon 8–9, 10
planets 8–9
Pluto 8–9
R
Rocket 8, 9, 10, 12
S
Satellite 12, 18

Saturn 8–9
Shuttle 11
solar eclipse 10
solar system 8–9
spacecraft 11
space exploration 11, 12, 18, 22–23
space station 12
spacewalk 12
Sputnik 10, 18
star 15
Sun 8–9
supernova 6
T
telescope 6
U
Universe, the 8–9
Uranus 8–9
V
V2 rocket 11
Venus 8–9

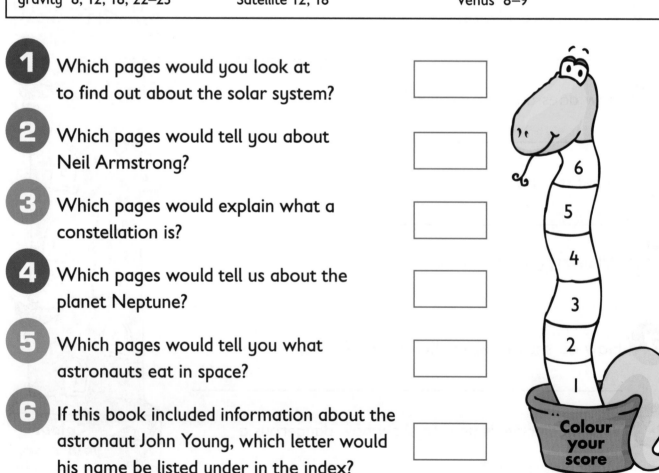

1 Which pages would you look at to find out about the solar system?

2 Which pages would tell you about Neil Armstrong?

3 Which pages would explain what a constellation is?

4 Which pages would tell us about the planet Neptune?

5 Which pages would tell you what astronauts eat in space?

6 If this book included information about the astronaut John Young, which letter would his name be listed under in the index?

6
5
4
3
2
1

Colour your score

Noun phrases

Underline the longest noun phrase in each sentence.

1. A silver helium balloon floated above the rooftops.

2. Your daft dog ran away with my shoe.

3. Sam was nervous about going to his new school.

4. Our goldfish have a shiny new tank.

5. The film was a comedy starring Tom Hanks.

6. My uncle has a parrot named Pete.

7. We all live in a yellow submarine.

8. Dad gave Mum a sparkling diamond ring when they got engaged.

9. We ordered four portions of cod and chips.

10. Dad bought a broken trombone at the auction by mistake.

11. I chose a book about the Ancient Greeks from the library.

12. A newly-formed girl band from Scotland won the talent competition.

13. Gran knitted me a ridiculously long, multi-coloured scarf.

14. Mum painted our garage door red.

A noun phrase can be replaced with a pronoun and still make sense.

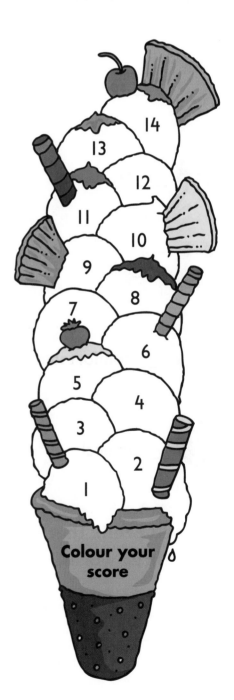

Colour your score

Prefixes

Choose the correct prefix to make a new word.

| un | dis | il | ir | mis |

The prefixes **un, dis** and **mis** have negative meanings.

1 ____sure

2 ____relevant

3 ____spell

4 ____legal

5 ____fair

6 ____comfortable

7 ____logical

8 ____usual

9 ____ability

10 ____understand

11 ____regular

12 ____advantage

13 ____fortune

14 ____responsible

Colour your score

| 15 |
| 14 |
| 13 |
| 12 |
| 11 |
| 10 |
| 9 |
| 8 |
| 7 |
| 6 |
| 5 |
| 4 |
| 3 |
| 2 |
| 1 |

Write a **prefix** that can be used in front of all three words.

15 _____ clockwise
social
freeze

16

Suffixes

Rewrite each **root word** adding the suffix **ion** or **ian**.

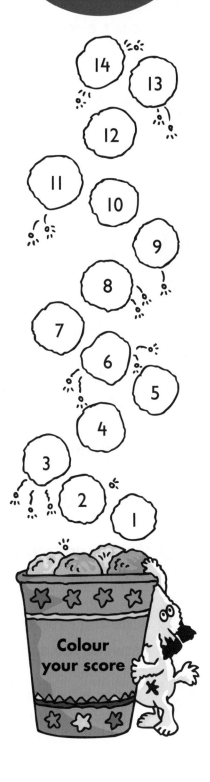

You may need to change or delete the last letter before adding the suffix.

1 invent   _____

2 magic   _____

3 discuss   _____

4 electric   _____

5 act   _____

6 music   _____

7 confess   _____

8 decorate   _____

9 confuse   _____

10 complete   _____

11 mathematics   _____

12 comprehend   _____

Choose a suitable **ion** or **ian** word to complete each sentence.

13 The _____ found the multiplication calculations easy.

14 The thief gave a full _____ to the police officer.

Colour your score

17

Homophones

Circle the correct word to complete each sentence.

1. I didn't mean to **break / brake** the plate.

2. The man held his stomach and began to **grown / groan**.

3. I can't **except / accept** this gift, it is too expensive.

4. Our team **won / one** the cup.

5. I got on the bus and paid my **fair / fare**.

6. The baby woke up and began to **ball / bawl**.

7. **Who's / Whose** shoes are those?

8. My dad had the biggest **piece / peace** of chocolate cake.

9. I couldn't tell **witch / which** of the paintings was fake.

10. The graze on my knee was **soar / sore**.

11. Mum bought me a **new / knew** skateboard.

12. We are not **aloud / allowed** to chew gum at school.

13. A **heard / herd** of angry looking cows stood between me and the gate.

14. Queen Elizabeth II's **rein / reign** is the longest of any British monarch.

Homophones sound the same but have different spellings and meanings.

Colour your score

14
13
12
11
10
9
8
7
6
5
4
3
2
1

Contractions

Write **your** or **you're** in each space.

1 Eat _____ vegetables!

2 Clean _____ teeth!

3 Make sure _____ always polite.

4 Always wash _____ hands before eating.

5 Take a break if _____ feeling tired.

6 Please put _____ plate in the dishwasher.

7 If _____ happy and you know it, clap

_____ hands!

Write **their** or **they're** in each space.

8 The puppies love _____ new home.

9 Hamsters store food in _____ cheeks.

10 The children will get extra play if _____
well behaved.

11 The class enjoyed meeting _____
new teacher.

12 Koalas are not bears; _____ marsupials.

13 Snakes shed _____ skin as they grow.

14 The twins aren't sure when _____ going

to get _____ exam results.

Your and **their**
are determiners;
you're and **they're**
are contractions.

14
13
12
11
10
9
8
7
6
5
4
3
2
1

**Colour your
score**

19

Adverbs and adverbials

Choose a suitable adverb to write in each space. Use each word once.

> Adverbs and adverbials tell us more about an action.

| constantly   reluctantly   tomorrow |
| silently   fortunately |

1 Billy, who hated vegetables, ate the soggy sprouts _____.

2 We tiptoed _____ past the sleeping baby.

3 Let's go to the beach _____.

4 _____, I have no homework this week.

5 The tap dripped _____.

Underline the adverbial in each sentence.

6 Timidly, Bobby opened the door to the head teacher's office.

7 The British cyclists finished first.

8 Taking great care, the antiques seller wrapped the vase.

9 The cat was hiding under the stairs.

10 Noah sang beautifully in the school concert.

11 We're going on holiday next week.

12 Anna manoeuvred her wheelchair through the busy shop.

Colour your score

Present perfect

Rewrite each sentence using the **present perfect** verb form.

Add **has** or **have** before the main verb.

1 Mum **washed** the car.

_____

2 I **read** The Jungle Book.

_____

3 We **visited** our cousins.

_____

4 It **snowed**.

_____

5 Mr Burgess **cleaned** the fish tank.

_____

_____

6 You **won**!

_____

7 My grandparents **went** on a cruise.

_____

_____

8 The votes **were** counted.

_____

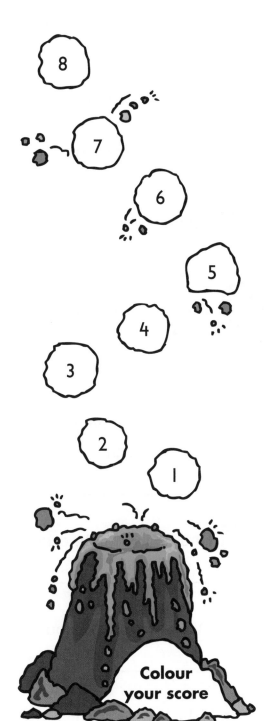

Colour your score

21

Comprehension: poetry

Read the poem to find an answer to each question.

Some One
By Walter de la Mare

Some one came knocking
   At my wee, small door;
Some one came knocking,
   I'm sure – sure – sure;
I listened, I opened,
   I looked to left and right,
But nought there was a-stirring
   In the still dark night;

Only the busy beetle
   Tap-tapping in the wall,
Only from the forest
   The screech-owl's call,
Only the cricket whistling
   While the dewdrops fall,
So I know not who came knocking,
   At all, at all, at all.

1 Find a word that means the same as 'small'.

_____

2 What does this mean: "But nought there was a-stirring"?

_____

3 Write three things that could be heard in the still dark night.

_____

4 Find and write an example of alliteration.

_____

5 What words can you find that rhyme with 'wall'?

_____

6 Which line has the most syllables?

_____

Colour your
score

22

Editing

Rewrite each sentence correcting any grammar or punctuation mistakes.

1 My uncle is a engineer.

_____

2 "I haven't done nothing!" declared Ryan.

_____

_____

3 We are moving to edinburgh.

_____

4 Sarah hasnt been on a plane before.

_____

_____

5 Harry and me do Judo on Saturdays.

_____

_____

6 The childrens' play area is closed today.

_____

_____

7 Your very clever!

_____

8 "Why are you late," asked the teacher.

_____

_____

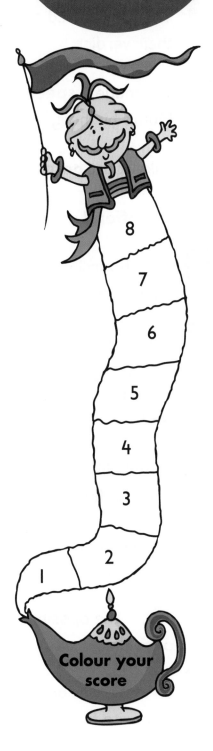

An editor checks writing for correct grammar, spelling and punctuation.

8
7
6
5
4
3
2
1

Colour your score

Common exception words

Circle the correct spelling.

1 It is important to eat a balanced diet and **exercize / exercise** regularly.

2 Helen is my aunt, **therefore / therefor** I am Helen's nephew.

3 The jury retired to **concider / consider** their verdict.

4 We made a **special / spacial** cake for Mum's birthday.

5 I like roast **potatoes / potatos** and gravy.

6 We **offen / often** go swimming in the sea.

7 Skateboarding is very **populer / popular** in my village.

8 I find it **difficult / dificult** to eat with chopsticks.

Underline the misspelled word and then write it correctly.

9 I would like to lern to play the flute. _____

10 I'm sertain I locked the door. _____

11 Hot is the oposite of cold. _____

12 Strawberries are my favourite frute. _____

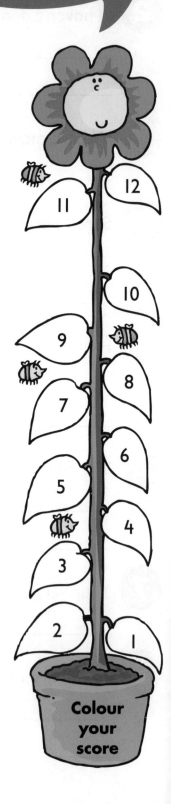

You need to learn the spellings of these words by heart.

12 11 10 9 8 7 6 5 4 3 2 1

Colour your score

24

Clauses

Put a tick or a cross to show if it is a clause or not.

1 seagulls watched us eating our chips ☐

2 the man in the moon ☐

3 Kenny the kangaroo ☐

4 I love my mum ☐

5 a timid mouse ☐

6 it rained all day ☐

7 my favourite colour is orange ☐

8 I don't like peas ☐

9 the church on the hill ☐

10 we always have chips on Fridays ☐

11 my tooth fell out yesterday ☐

12 my brother can't tie his shoelaces ☐

13 a funny joke ☐

14 I am ten years old ☐

15 my mum has blue hair ☐

A clause always has at least one noun or pronoun and a verb.

Colour your score

25

Linking clauses

Choose a suitable conjunction to link the clauses.

and but so or

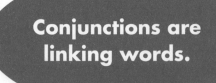

Conjunctions are linking words.

1 I put my ice cream in the freezer _____ it would not melt.

2 Please stop annoying me _____ I will tell Mum!

3 I like cartoons _____ Dad prefers sci-fi films.

4 I'm wearing sunglasses _____ the sun won't damage my eyes.

5 We're going to watch a film _____ then we will go for a pizza.

6 Would you like gravy _____ would you prefer ketchup?

7 I went to the library to change my book _____ I forgot my card.

8 Jim had a toothache _____ he went to the dentist.

9 Cinderella tried on the glass shoe _____ it was a perfect fit!

10 We wanted to go the museum _____ it was closed.

Colour your score

Subordinate clauses

Underline the **main clause** in each sentence.

1 Although I am tall for my age, I was too short to ride the rollercoaster.

2 Mum said she would drive me to school if I waited ten minutes.

3 No one has ever seen a real dinosaur because they became extinct long before humans lived on earth.

4 When we move house, I will no longer have to share a bedroom.

Underline the **subordinate clause** in each sentence.

5 Although they don't have legs, snakes can move very quickly.

6 Most lizards can shed their tails when they need to escape predators.

7 I turned off the TV because there was nothing worth watching.

8 Even though it looked delicious, Sam declined the cream cake.

9 Mum wanted to go on the zip wire whereas Dad did not.

10 I'd like to open an animal rescue centre when I grow up.

A subordinate clause does not make sense on its own.

Colour your score

10 9 8 7 6 5 4 3 2 1

Comprehension: non-fiction

Read the text to find an answer to each question.

Kensington Palace
June 7th 1836

My dearest Uncle,

I must thank you, my beloved Uncle, for the prospect of great happiness, you have contributed to give me, in the person of dear Albert. Allow me, then, my dearest Uncle, to tell you how delighted I am with him, and how much I like him in every way. He possesses every quality that could be desired to render me perfectly happy. He is so sensible, so kind, and so good, and so amiable too. He has besides, the most pleasing and delightful exterior and appearance, you can possibly see.

I have only now to beg you, my dearest Uncle, to take care of the health of one, now so dear to me, and to take him under your special protection. I hope and trust, that all will go on prosperously and well, on this subject of so much importance to me.

Believe me always, my dearest Uncle, your most affectionate devoted & grateful niece,

Victoria.

1 Does Victoria like her uncle? Explain your answer.

_____

2 What does "amiable" mean?

_____

3 What other "qualities" of Albert does Victoria mention in her letter?

_____

4 What two adjectives does Victoria use to describe Albert's appearance?

_____

5 What clue in the letter suggests that a member of the royal family wrote the letter?

_____

6 Which word in the letter means "thankful"?

_____

6

5

4

3

2

1

Colour your score

28

Possessive apostrophes

Add an **apostrophe** to each phrase to show possession.

1 Henrys jumper

2 The farmers dog

3 The wolves den

4 The ladies hockey team

5 Ellas book

Add **'s** to each irregular plural noun.

6 The children____ hospital ward

7 The men____ bathroom

8 The deer____ antlers

9 The cacti____ spines

10 The teeth____ enamel

Is the **apostrophe** used correctly?
Put a tick or a cross.

11 The twins' bedroom was very untidy. ☐

12 We have hedgehogs' in our garden. ☐

13 A hedgehog's prickles protect it from predators. ☐

14 Babies' nappies need changing frequently. ☐

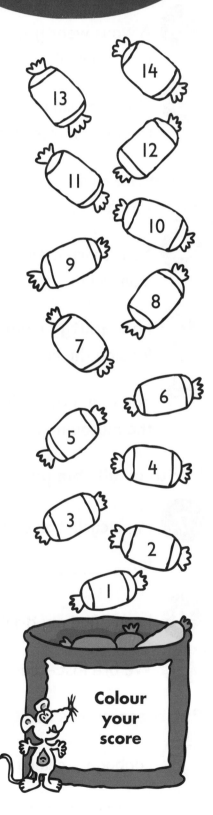

For plural nouns ending in s, add an apostrophe after the s.

Colour your score

Revision

Write a or an before each noun.

1 ____ aeroplane, ____ bicycle, ____ monorail

How many can you get right?

Add the missing speech punctuation.

2 Always wear your cycle helmet when you ride your bike said Dad.

3 My sister said I can't see the stage because the man in front is too tall.

Circle the best word in bold to complete each sentence.

4 Your story is **similar / different / unlike** from mine.

5 I am **guilty / responsible / important** for feeding the cat.

6 You may not **arrive / enter / entrance** the museum after six o'clock.

Write a suitable pronoun in each space.

7 My bicycle has a puncture – can you fix it

for _____?

8 I can't find my drink – have you seen _____?

9 We are lost – can you help _____?

Put these words in alphabetical order.

10 cabbage   celery   carrots

_____ _____ _____

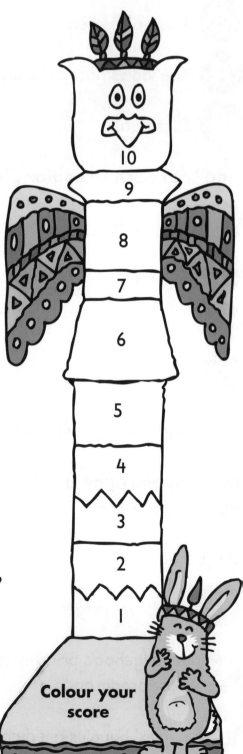

Colour your score

10
9
8
7
6
5
4
3
2
1

More revision

Add a prefix to make a word that has the opposite meaning.

1 _____behave, _____appear, _____legal

Rewrite each sentence using the **present perfect** verb form.

2 Ranulph Fiennes **climbed** Mount Everest.

_____

_____

3 Asma **learned** how to surf.

_____

4 We **went** to Snowdonia.

_____

Underline the **conjunction** in each sentence.

5 I put my model up high so my sister couldn't reach it.

6 Some snakes give birth to live babies but others lay eggs.

Underline the **subordinate clause** in each sentence.

7 We couldn't get to school because the snow was too deep.

8 Although moles are not blind, their eyesight is very poor.

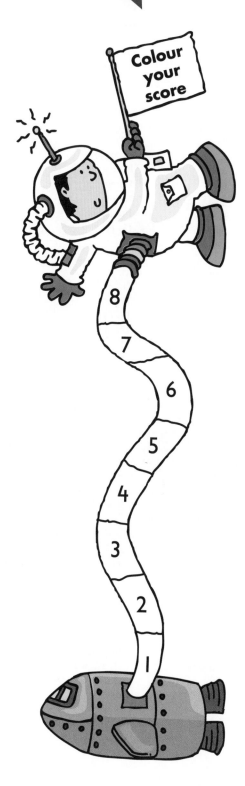

How quickly can you answer all the questions?

Colour your score

8
7
6
5
4
3
2
1

Answers

Comprehension: fiction
1. A horse / colt (Black Beauty)
2. Seven including Black Beauty
3. To run (fast)
4. Bad manners; kicking; biting
5. A race horse / a racing champion (he won twice at the Newmarket races)
6. Kind, gentle / good

Common exception words
1. bicycle
2. century
3. believe
4. breath
5. strange
6. library
7. separate
8. February
9. women
10. favourite
11. answer
12. minute
13. guard
14. notice
15. island

Consonants and vowels
1. r, l, t, s, x, z
2. e, o, u
3. ay
4. ey
5. y
6. ai
7. igh
8. ow
9. e
10. ough
11. ee
12. ea
13. ou
14. y
15. ei

A or an?
1. a
2. a
3. an
4. a
5. a
6. an
7. an
8. a
9. a
10. an
11. a
12. an
13. a
14. an
15. a

Direct speech
An exclamation mark may be used in place of a comma in questions 4, 7 and 8.
1. "Abracadabra!" shouted the magician.
2. "May I take your order?" asked the waiter.
3. The runner said, "I've got a blister."
4. "There's no place like home," said Dorothy.
5. Her brother yelled, "Go away!"
6. Tom asked, "Have you seen my car keys?"
7. "I'd like to go home," said the little boy.
8. "Bonjour," said Martine.

Choosing the best word
1. tall
2. stop
3. lifted
4. friendly
5. shouted
6. baking
7. short
8. increase
9. translate
10. lend
11. stained
12. narrow

Pronouns
1. we
2. it
3. he
4. she
5. they
6. I
7. us
8. they
9. them
10. it

First or third person?
1. First person
2. Third person
3. First person
4. Third person
5. First person
6. Third person
7. Third person
8. First person
9. First person
10. Third person
11. First person
12. First person

Biography
1. Albert
2. His
3. His
4. he
5. Albert
6. They
7. They
8. their
9. Albert and his family
10. their
11. they
12. Albert
13. He remembers
14. Albert's
15. him

Alphabetical order
1. ostrich puzzle quarter
2. newt octopus otter
3. yawn yogurt yolk
4. weather whale whistle
5. bonfire borrow bottom
6. suitcase sunflower supper
7. mirror money motorbike
8. iceberg ingredient insect
9. Algeria America Australia
10. kennel kettle kitten

Using a dictionary
1. It has short legs and neck, long grey fur and a striped head.
2. A sign people wear (to show they belong to a school or club)
3. As an adverb
4. backwards
5. badminton
6. back

Comprehension: non-fiction
1. Ears
2. They use their forked tongues / sense of smell
3. An animal that eats meat / other animals
4. By squeezing it so that it cannot breathe
5. Poison
6. In sacs close to the snake's fangs
7. Through their fangs
8. Deadly

Locating information
1. Pages 8–9
2. Pages 10, 11 and 12
3. Pages 15, 16 and 17
4. Pages 8–9
5. Pages 12 and 13
6. Y for 'Young' (people are listed under their last name)

Noun phrases
1. A silver helium balloon
2. Your daft dog
3. his new school
4. a shiny new tank
5. a comedy starring Tom Hanks
6. a parrot named Pete
7. a yellow submarine
8. a sparkling diamond ring
9. four portions of cod and chips
10. a broken trombone
11. a book about the Ancient Greeks
12. A newly-formed girl band from Scotland
13. a ridiculously long, multi-coloured scarf
14. our garage door

Prefixes
1. unsure
2. irrelevant
3. misspell
4. illegal
5. unfair
6. uncomfortable
7. illogical
8. unusual
9. disability
10. misunderstand
11. irregular
12. disadvantage
13. misfortune
14. irresponsible
15. anti

Suffixes
1. invention
2. magician
3. discussion
4. electrician
5. action
6. musician
7. confession
8. decoration
9. confusion
10. completion
11. mathematician
12. comprehension
13. mathematician
14. confession

Homophones
1. break
2. groan
3. accept
4. won
5. fare
6. bawl
7. Whose
8. piece
9. which
10. sore
11. new
12. allowed
13. herd
14. reign

Contractions
1. your
2. your
3. you're
4. your
5. you're
6. your
7. you're, your
8. their
9. their
10. they're
11. their
12. they're
13. their
14. they're, their